14.95

MW01388876

TOUCH

Wayne Jackman

Reading consultant:
Diana Bentley
University of Reading

Photographs by
Chris Fairclough

The Senses

Touch
Sight
Hearing
Smell
Taste

Editor: Janet De Saulles

First published in 1989 by
Wayland (Publishers) Ltd
61 Western Road, Hove
East Sussex, BN3 1JD, England

© Copyright 1989 Wayland (Publishers) Ltd

British Library Cataloguing in Publication Data
Jackman, Wayne
  Touch.
  1. Man. Touch – For children
  I. Title II. Series
  612'.88

  ISBN 1–85210–730–8

Phototypeset by Kalligraphics Ltd, Horley, Surrey, England
Printed and bound by Casterman S.A., Belgium

Contents

Touch is a sense	4
What does this feel like?	6
How do I feel things?	8
The brains behind the operation	11
What if we did not feel anything?	12
More about our nerves	14
Reflex actions	16
Tricking our sense of touch	18
Games for you and your friends	20
Glossary	22
Books to read	23
Index	24

All the words that appear in **bold** are explained in the glossary on page 22.

Touch is a sense.

There are five **senses** — sight, touch, smell, hearing and taste. This book is about touch. Look around you. How many different things can you see? Reach out and touch some of them. Are they hard or wet, smooth or cold, or rough? They all have a different feel. You can feel them because of your sense of touch.

What does this feel like?

Some things are nice to touch but other things can feel strange. Have you ever tried to pick up a wriggly worm? How long did you manage to hold it? Perhaps you like being tickled with a soft feather. Other feelings can be useful. Our body warns us when our skin gets overheated or too cold. Can you see that the boy in the picture opposite is too hot?

How do I feel things?

Our skin covers all our body. It contains **nerves**. Each nerve picks up different types of feelings. Where the nerves are close together our skin is very sensitive, like on our hands, lips, and the soles of our feet. Our feet, for example, can feel even the tiniest pebble. Our backs and bottoms are not so sensitive because the nerves are far apart.

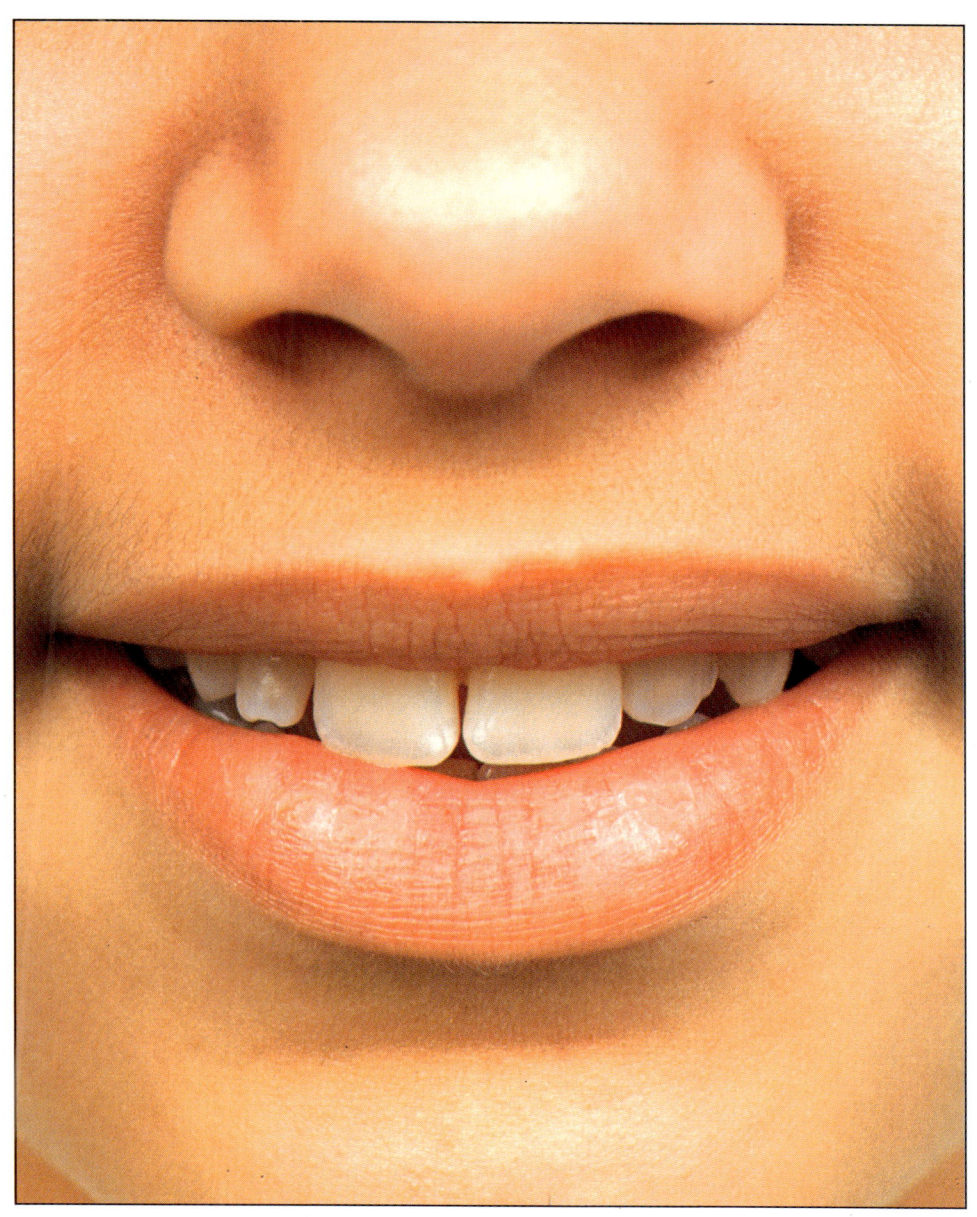

The brains behind the operation.

Our skin is made up of different layers. The layer on the outside of the body is dead. It is called the **epidermis**. It may have a dark colour or a pale colour. Underneath there is another layer which is alive. This is called the **dermis**. It is where the ends of the nerves are. Each of these nerves takes messages of what it can feel up to the **brain**. We then know what we are touching.

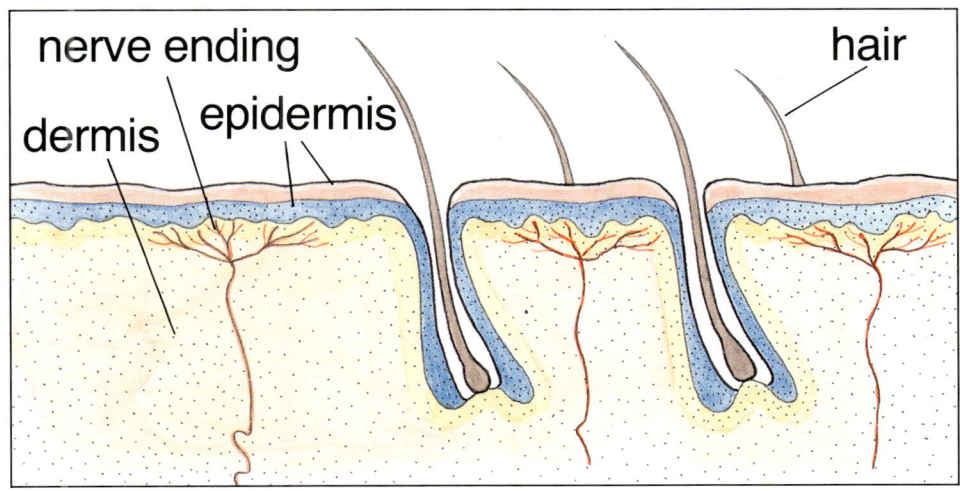

What if we did not feel anything?

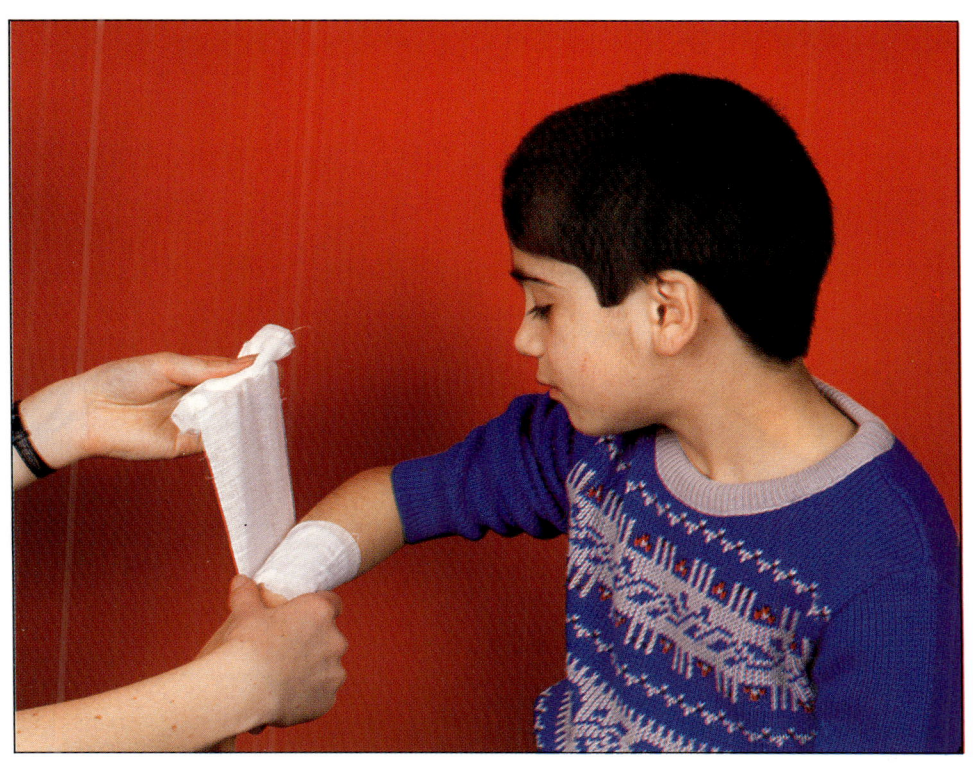

Have you ever slept with your arm in a funny position? Perhaps you woke up with a **numb** feeling in it. It would be dangerous if our body was always like that. If we could not feel anything, we might burn ourselves by drinking soup which is too hot. We might even cut ourselves badly and not notice.

More about our nerves.

After some people have had bad accidents, their nerves may be damaged. This can mean that when they touch something – even the sharp thorn of a rose, for example – they cannot feel it. Their nerves are not sending the message to their brains.

Now try this experiment to see how easily your nerves recognize hot and cold. Take a piece of silver foil. Touch it. Does it feel cold? Now breathe on it. It should feel warm.

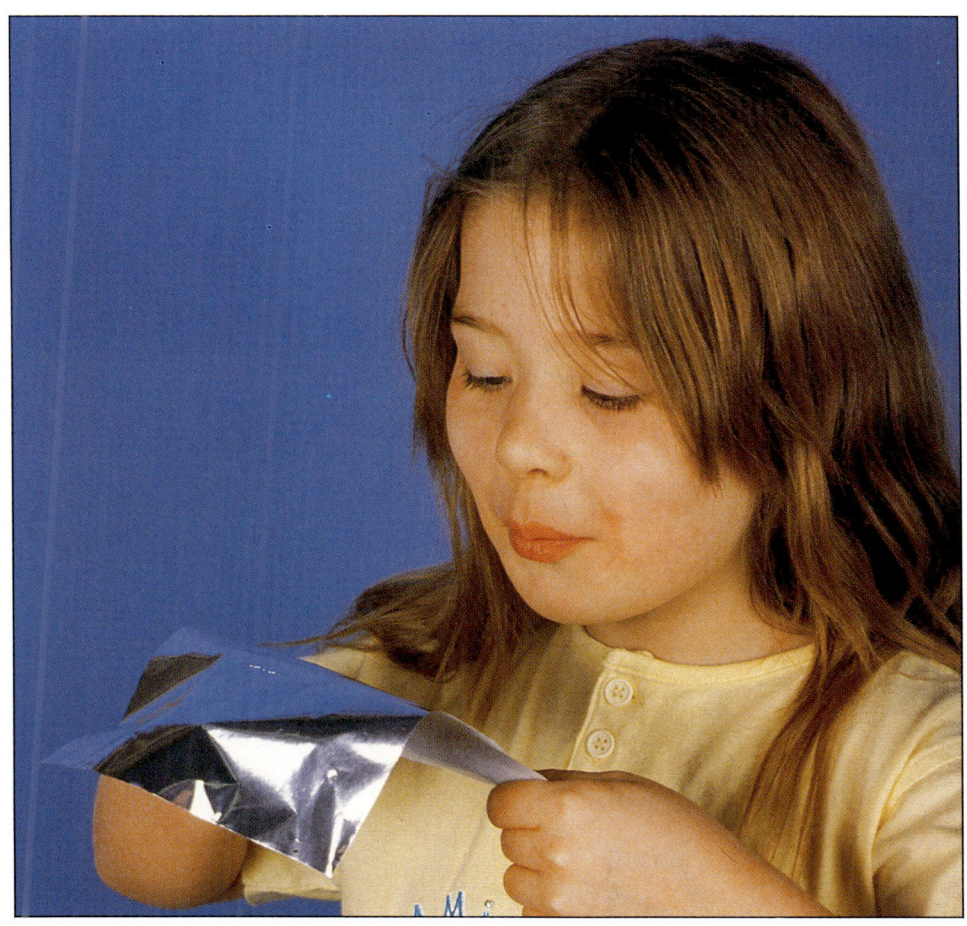

Reflex actions.

Have you ever picked up a baked potato or a very hot plate and dropped it straight away? When you do this, it is because the nerves send a message directly to your arm muscles. You let go of the hot object at once, as a **reflex action**. Our sense of touch keeps us safe.

Tricking our sense of touch.

Remember that we said our backs are not very sensitive? Gently touch a friend's back with the blunt end of a pencil. Now use two pencils close together. If the pencils are not more than about 2 cm apart, the person may still think it is only one pencil.

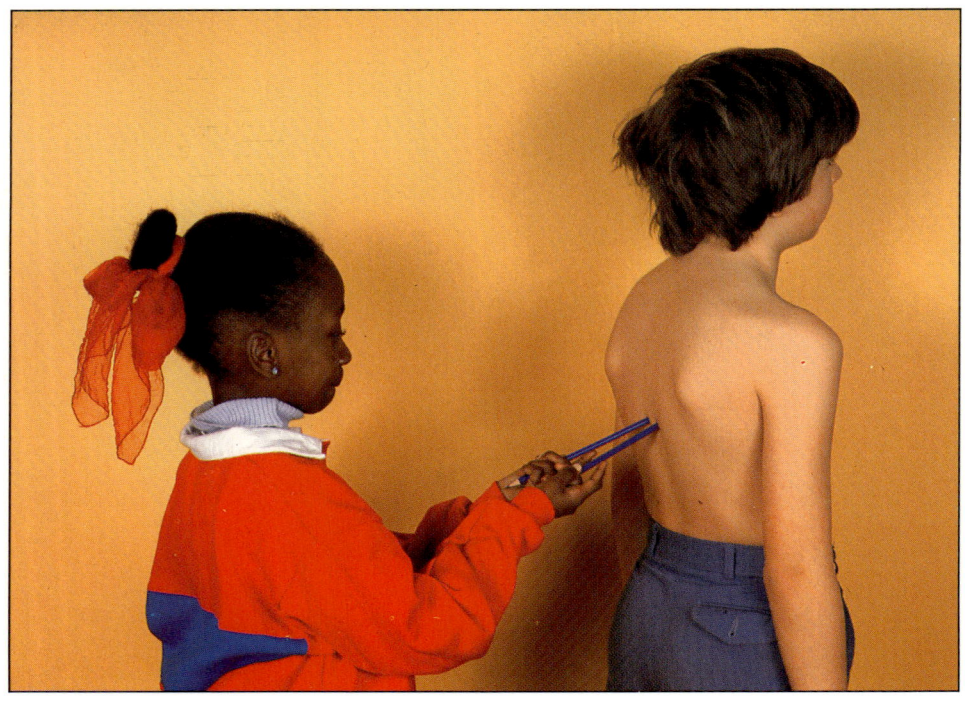

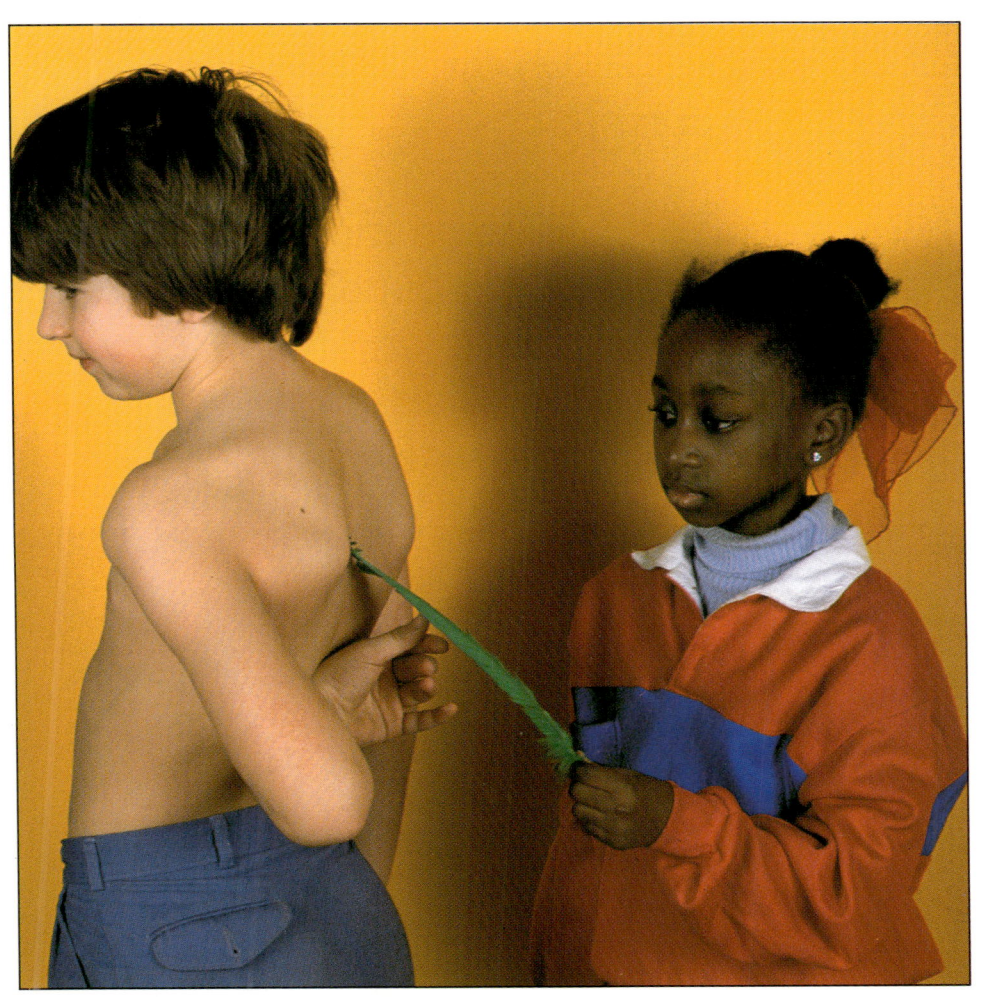

This time use a feather. The person being tickled scratches the spot where he or she thinks the tickle is. It is very hard to find it!

Games for you and your friends.

1. Tie a scarf around someone's eyes. Spin the blindfolded person around and then ask him or her to recognize everyone by touching and feeling their faces. This is one way that blind people get to know new people.

2. Cut a hole in each end of a cardboard box. One person feeds things into the box. A friend sits with his or her eyes closed at the other end. The friend puts both hands inside the box and guesses what is in it. Use things like cold cooked spaghetti or a bag of squashy jelly!

Glossary

Brain   The brain is the part of the body which controls and organizes the way we act, think and speak.

Dermis   The layer of skin found under the epidermis. It is where the nerve endings are.

Epidermis   The outside layer of skin which protects us from germs and dirt.

Nerves   The cords which send messages from different parts of the body to the brain.

Numb   When a part of the body cannot feel anything.

Reflex action   When the nerves send a message to the right part of the body without the brain needing to think at all. The brain only receives the message after we have already acted.

Senses   We use our senses to know what things look, feel, smell, sound and taste like.

Books to read

I Touch With My Fingers by Joan Mills (Schofield & Son, 1986)

Things I Touch illustrated by Peter Longden (Ladybird, 1985)

Touching by Henry Pluckrose (Franklin Watts, 1985)

Your Hands and Feet by Joan Iveson-Iveson (Wayland, 1985)

Your Skin and Hair by Joan Iveson-Iveson (Wayland, 1985)

Acknowledgements

The author and Publisher would like to thank the Headteacher, staff and pupils of Millfield Junior School, Elmcroft Street, London, for their help in producing this book.

Index

Accident 14
Arm 13, 16

Back 8, 18
Blind 20
Body 8, 11, 13
Bottom 8
Brain 11, 14

Cold 4, 6, 15

Dermis 11

Epidermis 11
Eyes 21

Face 20
Feeling 4, 6, 8, 11, 12, 13, 14, 15, 20
Feet 8

Hands 8, 21
Hearing 4
Hot 6, 13, 15, 16

Lips 8

Muscles 16

Nerves 8, 11, 14, 16
Numb 13

Sense 4
Sight 4
Skin 8, 11
Smell 4

Taste 4
Tongue 8
Touch 4, 6, 8, 14, 15, 16

Warm 15